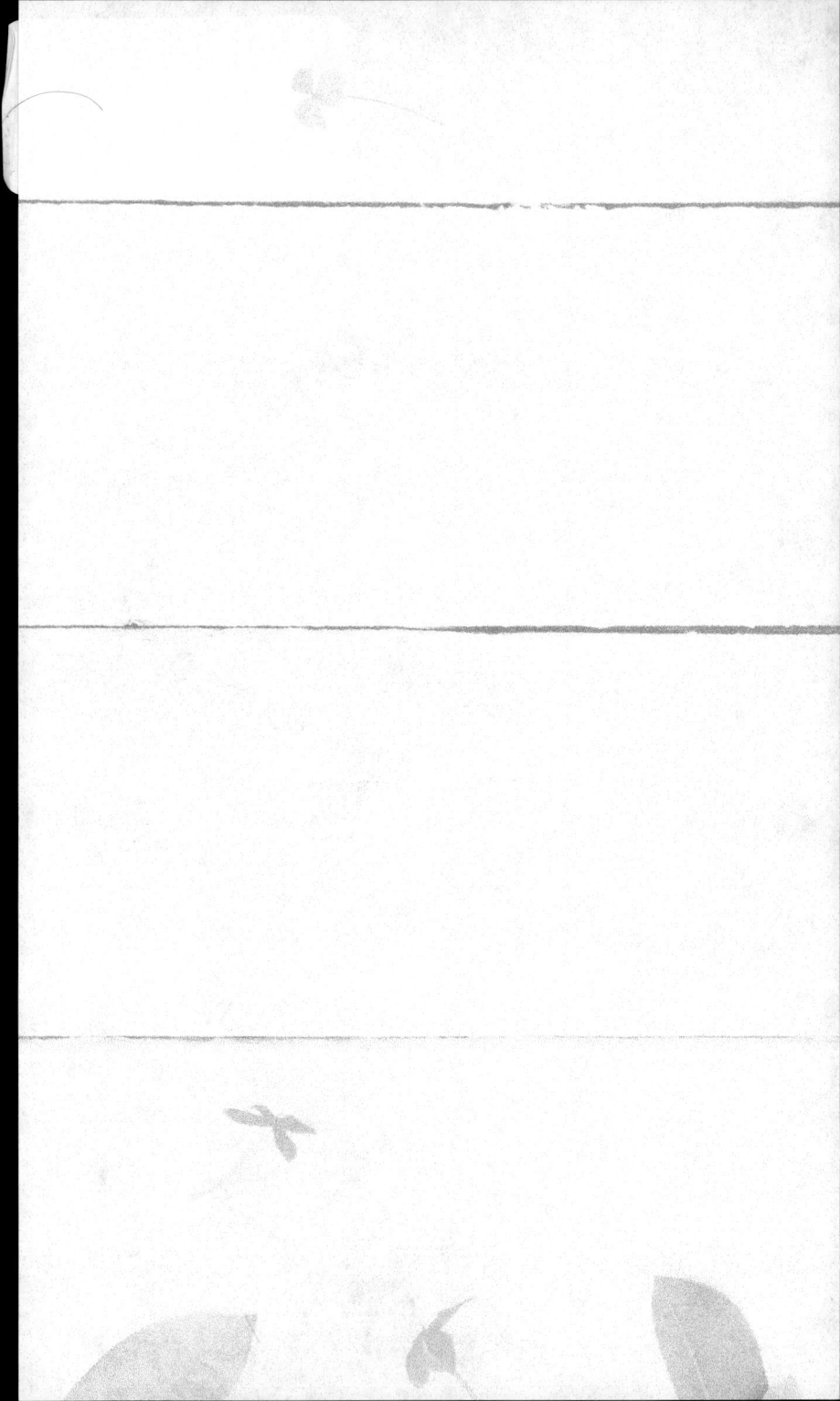

FRIENDS GIFT
SERIES

Good Gift Books
and Merchandise™

Family is essential for survival. Friends are essential for surviving our family.

Thadeus Blackwell

Note from the Editor

If you are lucky enough to be a recipient of this book, a congratulations are in order. This means that you have a friend who undoubtedly cares deeply about you, and that is not something that should ever be taken for granted. Over the last few years, study after study has shown that loneliness does far more than affect our quality of life; it can also be detrimental to our physical health and wellbeing. This is particularly troubling as we as a society continue to build walls between us and other humans, choosing instead to interact with technological devices, most of which were, ironically, intended to help us connect with other humans.

It's crucial that we reverse this trend, and hopefully, this book will play a small part in deepening your bond with the lovely person who gifted you this book. It is my sincere hope that the words in this book reflect the deepness of your friendship, and that this very special relationship will endure and deepen for many years to come.

Enjoy!

— Violet Jade

In our lives we have our crew, a group of friends to help us through ...

The crew is great, but soon we knew there's something special between me and you.

For reasons
I still can't
comprehend,
the two of us
became best
friends.

We talked and
talked,

it never grew old.

No topic off limits,

no joke untold.

And with
this gift,
what I aim
to do ...

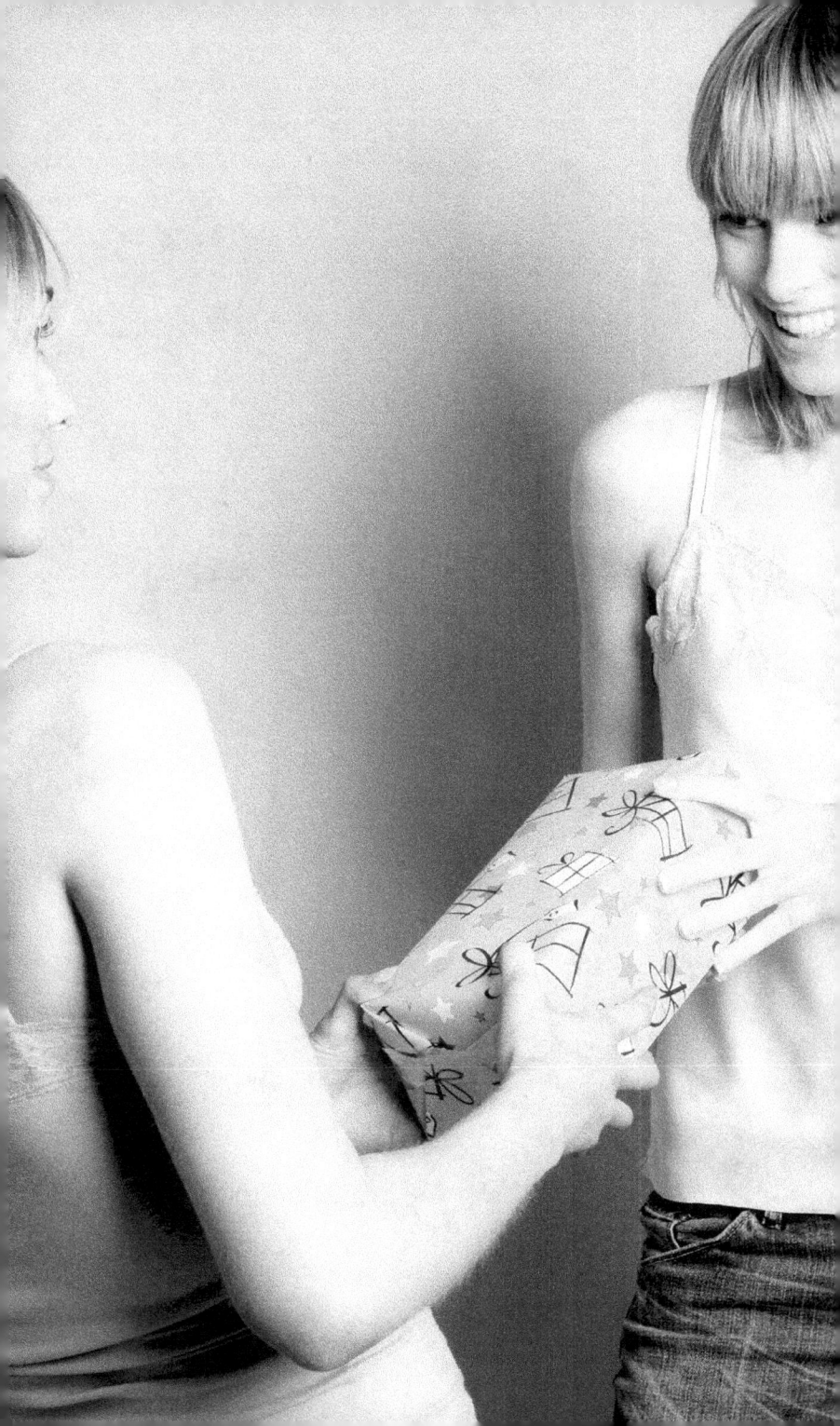

Is to express
the ways I
appreciate you.

Like how you

comfort when

I'm feeling

blue ...

And how you
find fun things
to do.

With you,
all is better,
even when
life is
mundane ...

Like the
time we got
stuck out in
the rain.

Or the time
when you let
me share your
drink ...

And when I
was too sad
to speak.

Or that
time you
reminded
me to
bring a
sweater ...

Or the time
you told
me that I
deserved
better.

Or the times

we heeded to

have a brutal

conversation ...

Or the times
we dressed
all wrong for
the occasion.

And even
when what
happened
was what
we'd
feared ...

And when
that party
just got
weird.

And looking back at how we used to dress ...

And at
all the
ease, and
all the
stress ...

For you,
I have
but one
request:

Tell me, how do I look in this dress?

You're the
only one
I can ask
without
fear ...

Who will tell
me what I
need to hear.

Besides,
along this
life's
scenic
route ...

It's obvious that we look cute.

Sure,

we butt

heads

every

now and

then ...

But I
never
wonder
whose
corner
you're in.

And no one
will come
between us
two ...

And I
pity the
person who
says mean
things about
you!

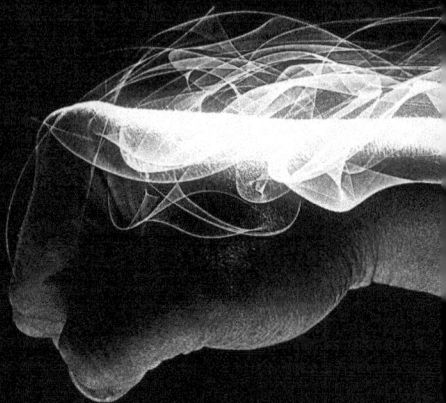

When
I need
help ...

I don't have to ask,

Even when
it's an
unpleasant
task.

You help
me keep
my life on
track ...

And I
always know
you've got
my back.

You always
know just
how to
respond ...

And no
one else
quite
"gets" our
bond.

And as
you read
through
this
string of
rhymes ...

Think

back

upon

those

lovely

times

...

There's been:

dancing ...

And dancing ...

And dancing ...

And there's
more to do ...

And I don't
know what
I'd do
without you.

And when
I think
about what
we've been
through ...

It reminds me how much ...

I
love
you!

And I
know that
our good
times are
far from
done ...

More
memories
to make
for years
to come!

We hope you've enjoyed your copy of Best Friend Ever! Hopefully this book has helped express feelings of love between you and a very special person in your life.